LET'S PLAY A RHYME

READY-TO-USE RHYMES
TO PROMOTE EARLY LEARNING SKILLS

by Christine Branch

Incentive Publications, Inc.
Nashville, Tennessee

Illustrated by Gayle Seaberg Harvey
Cover by Marta Drayton
Edited by Jan Keeling

Library of Congress Catalog Card Number: 94-75266
ISBN 0-86530-288-X

PRINTED IN THE UNITED STATES OF AMERICA

Table of Contents

Preface

To My Friends Who Play These Rhymes:

I am sure you enjoy times full of fun with people you love. *Let's Play a Rhyme* has been written for the busy mother, caretaker, and preschool teacher who wants to share big learning adventures with little people. These ready-made rhymes promote growth and development while sparking in children an enthusiasm for learning. Listening, thinking, and speaking skills are combined with activities that develop the early learner's fine and gross motor skills. The rhymes are simple to learn and can be played with children anytime you have a few minutes together.

Each verse includes actions you can pantomime. The verses have been formatted with the rhyme on the left-hand side of the page and the suggested actions to accompany the rhymes on the right-hand side of the page. I hope you will use your imaginations to come up with new ideas for the motions. Sometimes you may want to use big, noisy actions. Other times it is best to play the rhymes quietly in your lap. Whatever you decide to do, make it fun!

Sincerely,

Christine Branch

Today Is My Birthday

Today is my birthday.
How old can I be?   (Point to yourself.)
You'll guess the secret
If you play with me.

We'll mix up a cake,   (Mix.)
Wait while it bakes,   (Put your palm on your chin.)
Mix up the frosting,   (Mix.)
See how it tastes.   (Taste.)

What flavor is it?
I'll give you a clue.   (Count the flavors.)
There's chocolate, cherry,
Strawberry, too,
Lemon, or butterscotch,
To name a few.

Now, candles on top.
How old can I be?   (Put on the candles.)
Strike this match.
We'll light them and see.   (Light the candles.)

One, Two, Three . . .   (How high can you count?)

The Choo Choo Train

(Can you tell directions? Which is left? Which is right?)

Chug-Chug, Chug-Chug,   (Move your arms around.)
Toot! Toot!   (Pull the whistle as you
                               march in place.)

All aboard the choo choo train. (Motion aboard.)
Please sit down.   (Motion to the seat.)
I'm glad you came.   (Bow low.)
First turn left.   (Move your arms around
                               and march left.)

Chug up the hill.   (Chug slowly.)
Then turn right   (March to the right.)
    around the mill.
Faster, faster, down we go.   (Speed up.)
There's a bridge.   (Point to the bridge.)
Bend down low.   (Bend down.)
Now turn left beside the sea. (Turn left.)
Please slow down
    or wet we'll be.   (Slow down.)
Now turn right.   (Turn right.)
We're at the end.
Chug-Chug-Chug!   (March in place.)
Let's do it again!

Toot! Toot!   (Pull the whistle.)

Shoe-Tying Rhyme

(Practice tying a shoe while repeating the verse.)

Watch the trick I've got for you.
I've learned how to tie my shoe.

Take a shoelace in each hand.
Make them cross. I think I can.

Then, I tuck the top lace through.
Pull them tight, that's what to do.

Hold the left lace in left hand.
With the right, a loop will stand.

Wrap the left lace 'round right thumb.
Hold that loop until I'm done.

Touch left lace in back of thumb.
Push it through. This is fun.

Pull both loops 'til they are tight.
Now the bow is made just right.

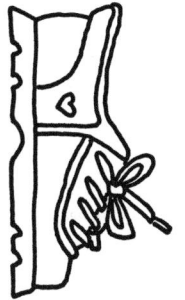

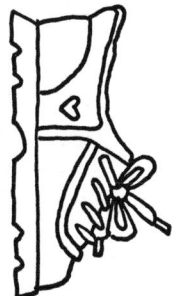

Swinging Song

**(As you swing, pump your feet in and out
and say the verse.)**

Sing a little swinging song,
sing and swing,
sing and swing.

Sing a little swinging song,
and sing,
and sing,
and swing.

Jumping Rope

(Use a real or pretend rope. How high can you count?)

Jump rope! Jump rope!
Jump with me!

Jump rope! Jump rope!
One! Two! Three!

First jump fast.
Then jump slow.

Make my jump rope
Go! Go! Go!

One! Two! Three! Four! . . .

The Parade

(Will you join our parade? What instrument will you play?)

As we start down the street,	(March in place.)
Hear our march, march, feet!	
Hear our shiny cymbals crash!	(Clap your hands.)
Smash! Smash! Smash!	
Hear the tambourine pat,	(Pat your hand.)
The drum tat-a-tat.	(Play a drum.)
Hear the horn toot, toot.	(Play a horn.)
You might hear a flute.	(Play a flute.)
Hear the bell ding, ding,	(Ring a bell.)
The triangle ring.	(Play the triangle.)
See the flags flap, flap,	(Wave a flag.)
The people clap, clap.	(Clap your hands.)
As we march down the street,	(March in place.)
Hear our march, march, feet!	

Painter of Rainbows

(Can you recognize each color? Paint a rainbow.)

We're painters of rainbows, you and I.
We splash our colors across the sky.

Red, sweet as strawberries, apples, and
    cherries.
Orange, hot as peppers, sunsets, and poppies.
Yellow, as mellow as ducklings and chicks.
Green, tart as pickles, lime sherbet, Popsicles.
Blue, cool as sea spray, mountains, and
    fountains.
Purple, fragrant as periwinkle and plums.

We're painters of rainbows, you and I.
With buckets of color, we're painting the sky.

Jelly Beans

(This rhyme is fun to do with a jump rope.)

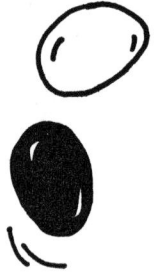

Jelly Beans,	**(Hop on your right foot.)**
Jelly Beans,	**(Hop on your left foot.)**
In a	**(Hop on your right foot.)**
Jar.	**(Hop on your left foot.)**

How many	**(Hop on your right foot.)**
Beans do you	**(Hop on your left foot.)**
Think there	**(Hop on your right foot.)**
Are?	**(Hop on your left foot.)**
One, Two, Three, Four . . .	**(Jump on both feet.)**

Jelly Beans,	**(Right Foot)**
Jelly Beans,	**(Left Foot)**
In a	**(Right Foot)**
Dish.	**(Left Foot)**

What color	**(Right Foot)**
Jelly Beans	**(Left Foot)**
Do you	**(Right Foot)**
Wish?	**(Left Foot)**
Pink, Blue, Red . . .	**(Jump on both feet while taking turns saying different colors.)**

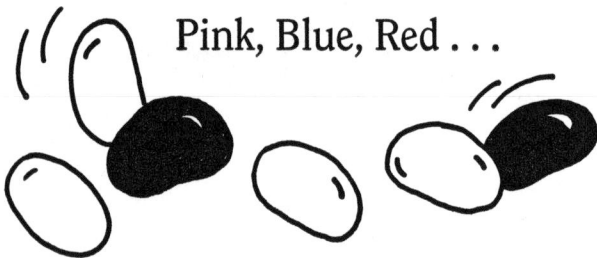
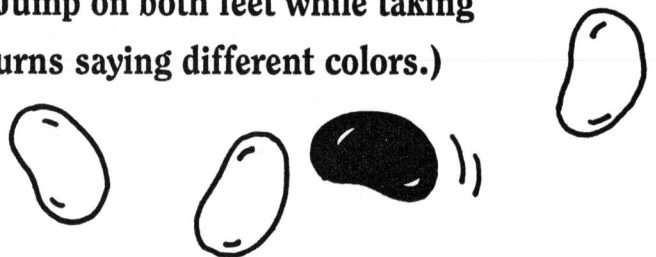

Playing the Alphabet

(Write the letters in the air or pantomime actions.)

Playing the alphabet is fun to do.
Especially when I play it with you.

A is for ABLE to skip, hop, and run.   **(Skip, hop, and run.)**

B is for BALL BOUNCING.
It's so much fun.   **(Bounce a ball.)**

C is for CIRCLE, big fat and round.   **(Make a circle.)**

D is for DOG. My faithful, old   **(Pet dog.)**
hound.

E is for EAST, the opposite of west.   **(Point east and west.)**

F is for FRIEND; you are the best.   **(Point to your friend.)**

G is for GIANT. I've seen one or   **(Raise your arms over**
two.   **your head.)**

H is for HUG. I have one for you.   **(Hug yourself.)**

I is for ICE CREAM, my favorite   **(Lick a cone.)**
thing.

J is for JINGLE, and all bells that   **(Ring a bell.)**
ring.

K is for KITTEN. Mine's soft and   **(Pet your hand.)**
warm.

L is for LIGHTNING that comes   **(Flutter your fingers**
in a storm.   **down.)**

M is for MARSHMALLOW, melt in my mouth.   **(Pop one in your mouth.)**

N is for NORTH, opposite south.   **(Point north and south.)**

O is for ORANGE, juicy and sweet.   **(Rub your tummy.)**

P is for PARROT and PARAKEET.   **(Rest your elbow on your other hand.)**

Q is for QUEEN with a gold crown.   **(Touch your head.)**

R is for RACE, run all over town.   **(Run in place.)**

S is for SHIP, way out in space.   **(Push your hand quickly into the air.)**

T is for TURTLE, with a poky pace.   **(Move your hand slowly.)**

U is for UPHILL, a very hard climb.   **(Climb in place.)**

V is for VALENTINE. Will you be mine?   **(Point to your friend.)**

W is for WIGGLE. I'm good at that.   **(Wiggle.)**

X is for X-RAY. A bone photograph.   **(Take a picture.)**

Y is for YELLOW, my favorite balloon.   **(Shape hands in a circle.)**

Z is for ZOOM as I land on the moon.   **(Fall down and fold your arms.)**

Autumn

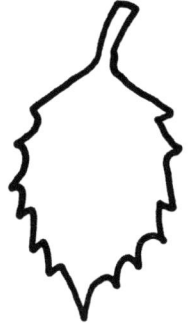

Birds fly away to
    warmer lands.

**(Repeatedly touch thumb and
fingers of your left hand, while
making your arm fly.)**

I pull mittens on
    my hands.

(Pull on mittens.)

We rake leaves:
    brown, red, gold.

(Rake the leaves.)

I zip my coat to
    keep out cold.

(Zip your coat.)

Crispy apples,
    chicken soup,

(Pretend to eat.)

I pull on my new
    red boots.

(Pull on boots.)

Fat, ripe pumpkin,

(Put arms in a circle, down low.)

Harvest moon,

(Put arms in a circle, up high.)

Halloween
    will be here soon!

When It Rains

When the rain makes puddles,	(Flutter fingers down.)
here a puddle, there.	(Point to puddles.)
I jump in the puddles.	(Clap your hands.)
They splash everywhere.	(Wave your arms.)
My rainboots squish	
as I climb up the hill.	(Climb in place.)
I hold my hat	
when the wind blows chill.	(Hold your hat.)
But if it should thunder,	(Roll your arms.)
I run inside,	(Run in place.)
And quickly find a place	
to hide.	(Hands over head.)

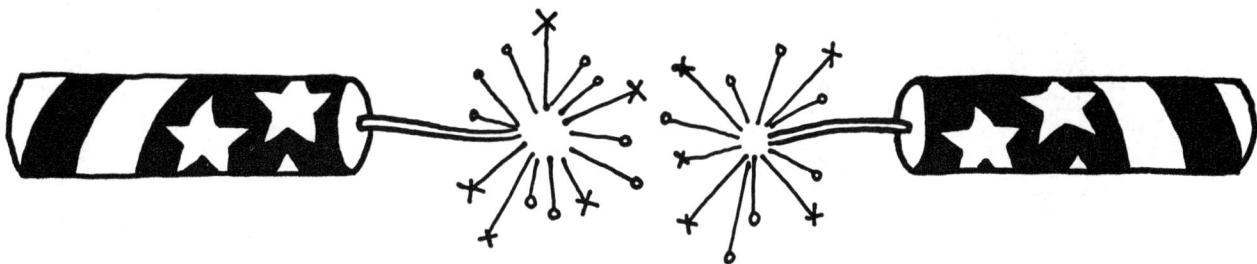

Cheerleader Cheer

Firecracker, Firecracker,   **(Do jumping jacks.)**
   Boom! Boom! Boom!   **(Clap hands.)**
Kick up your heels   **(Put your hands on your waist.)**
   and give us some room!   **(Kick your legs.)**
We'll spin you   **(Twirl with your arms out.)**
   and we'll win you
   and we'll blast you to   **(Put one fist up.)**
   the moon!

Get 'um!   **(Roll your arms.)**
Get 'um!
Get 'um!
Go!   **(Raise your fist, jump.)**

The Scarecrow

Five fat blackbirds,
Sitting in the straw,   (Hold up five fingers.)

Laughing at the scarecrow.   (Use thumb and fingers
Caw! Caw! Caw!   for the bird's beak.)

Five fat blackbirds,
Eating all the corn.   (Scratch the ground.)

Silly old birds,   (Shake your finger.)
It's going to storm.   (Wiggle your fingers.)

Poor sad scarecrow   (Look sad.)
Sitting on the fence.   (Rest your right elbow
                                             on your left arm.)

"Boo!" yelled the scarecrow.   (Clap your hands.)
Away they went!   (Hide your hand behind
                                             your back.)

Lonely Little Pumpkin

Lonely little pumpkin
    in the pumpkin patch,   **(Make a circle with your arms.)**
I can cheer you up,   **(Trace your smile.)**
    just like that.   **(Snap your fingers.)**

I'll cut a round hat,   **(Cut a hat.)**
    scoop out the seeds.   **(Scoop out the seeds.)**
A jack-o'-lantern smile
    is just what you need.   **(Trace your smile.)**

A funny-shaped nose,   **(Point to your nose.)**
    two scary eyes—   **(Point to your eyes.)**
You get to be   **(Point to the pumpkin.)**
    my Halloween surprise.   **(Point to yourself.)**

I'll lift up your hat,   **(Lift hat.)**
    put in a light.   **(Hold one finger like a candle, resting it in the palm of the other hand.)**

Now you are ready
    for trick or treat night!

Halloween Spooks

(Can you count backwards? This rhyme will help you.)

10 white ghosts floating through the air.   **(Make ghostly floating motions.)**

9 cackling witches give me a scare.   **(Put your hands on your cheeks.)**

8 black cats, you'd better beware.   **(Shake your finger.)**

7 goofy goblins without a care.   **(Dance and wave your arms.)**

6 spooky vampires prickle my hair.   **(Hold your head.)**

5 black bats flying everywhere.   **(Repeatedly touch thumb and fingers while moving arm.)**

4 moaning monsters, specimens rare.   **(Hold up your claws.)**

3 strange spacemen, stop to stare.   **(Put your hand over your eyes.)**

2 pretty gypsies, dance where they dare.   **(Dance in a circle, wave your arms.)**

1 little me, hides under a chair!   **(Crouch down with your hands over your head.)**

Boooooooooo!

Four Orange Pumpkins

Three orange pumpkins	(Hold up three fingers.)
knocked on a witch's door.	(Knock.)
Another rolled along	(Roll your arms.)
and that made four.	(Hold up four fingers.)
The first was happy	(Hold up one finger.)
with a toothless grin.	
The second was sad;	(Hold up two fingers.)
he needed a friend.	
The third orange pumpkin	(Hold up three fingers.)
was tall and thin.	
The fourth was scary.	(Wiggle your baby finger.)
Don't let him in.	
Then, the funny little witch	(Wiggle your thumb.)
said,	
"Where have you been?"	(Grab all the fingers.)

A Time for Thanksgiving

A time for thinking . . .   (Touch your
    about good things,   head.)
    like food, and home, and friends.

A time for wishing . . .   (Touch your
    for a world,   chest.)
    with peace that never ends.

A time for hoping . . .   (Put your hands
    for the best.   together.)
    May all people soon be free.

A time for sharing . . .   (Hold your
    what we have.   hands out.)
    That's how it's meant to be.

The Sneaky Snitcher

Grandma's pumpkin pies are almost done.   (Hold your hands in a circle, sniff.)

Mama's yummy rolls are minus one.   (Take a roll, put it behind your back.)

Grandpa carves the turkey.   (Carve the turkey.)

Auntie sets the table.   (Set the table.)

Daddy watches football, he'd help if he were able.   (Hold your hands in circles in front of your eyes.)

All the rest sit and wait, hungry as can be.   (Rest your chin on your hand, rub your tummy.)

Except for one sneaky snitcher,   (Take out your roll, eat it.)

That's Me!   (Point to yourself.)

On Snowy Nights

On snowy nights when cold
    winds blow,   (Flutter your fingers down.)
All our lights are turned down
    low.
Warm brown cocoa in my cup—   (Drink your cocoa.)
By the fire, I drink it up.
Hear the popcorn.   (Turn your palms up and
    Pop! Pop! Pop!   flex your fingers.)
I dance with it.
    Hop! Hop! Hop!   (Hop up and down.)
Read a story, snuggily warm.   (Hold your hands like a
                            book. Hug yourself.)
I wish it would always storm.   (Flutter your fingers down.)

Puppy's Question

Falling, falling softly down,
    fluffy snowflakes to the ground.

Diamond sparkles everywhere,
    on the roof and branches bare.

Puppy barks and looks at me
    as if to say, "How can it be?"

I've figured out the reason,
    though.
    My playful pup will never know.

It must be angels way up high,
    having pillow fights in the sky.

(What do you think causes the snow?)

**(Reach hands above head
and touch the ground.)**

**(Touch fingertips like a
roof. Stretch out arms
and twirl in a circle.)**
(Shrug your shoulders.)

**(Put your finger to your
forehead.)**

**(Point to the sky.
Swing your pillow.)**

Mr. Snowman

One!	(Scoop up snow and make balls.)
Two!	
Three!	
Big cold snowballs,	
if you please.	
I will stack them way	
up high.	
Mr. Snowman, reach	(Reach up high. Stack them up.)
the sky.	
Rocks for eyes, carrot	(Put on the eyes and nose.)
nose,	
A stick for an arm	(Put on his arms.)
in each side goes.	
My hat and gloves,	(Dress the snowman.)
then we're through.	
Brrrrrrr!	(Shiver and hug yourself.)
I think I need them	
more than you!	(Take back your hat and gloves.)

Sleigh Ride

Crunch! Crunch! Crunch!	(Hike with big steps.)
We hike the snowy hill.	
Huff! Puff! Puff!	(Keep marching.)
Our noses feel the chill.	(Rub your nose.)
At the top,	
we climb onto the sled.	(Climb onto your sled.)
Oops! Be careful!	
Don't fall off on your head!	(Almost fall off.)
Whiz! Whiz! Whiz!	(Guide your sled.)
Don't run into that tree!	(Point to the tree.)
Crash! Bang! Bump!	(Cover your eyes.)
Hey! Get off of me!	(Fall off the sled.)

The Christmas Present

Underneath our Christmas Tree,   (Touch your fingertips together.)
  there's a box
  addressed to me.   (Point to yourself.)
The brightly colored paper
  is tied up with a bow.   (Make the bow loops.)
And what could be inside it,
  I'm sure I don't know.   (Shrug your shoulders.)
When nobody   (Hold your hand out over your
  is looking,   eyes.)
  I sneak under the tree.   (Sneak on tiptoe.)
I shake it and I squeeze it.   (Shake and squeeze it.)
  Oh, my! What could it be?   (Put your hands on your cheeks.)
A doll, a ball,   (Rock the doll, shape the ball,
  a teddy bear?   and hug the bear.)
  Maybe just some   (Hold up clothing,
  underwear.   pull your face.)
I think I'll wrap one   (Wrap the present.)
  just for you.
Now, I have a secret, too!

(What is your secret?)

The Christmas Tree

(Can you help put each decoration on the tree?)

Help me decorate the tree
    with Christmas magic all can see.
First, the lights that blink so bright,
    making twinkles when it's night.
Then glass balls, blue, red, and green,
    and gingerbread cookies in between.
Toy soldier, clown, and rocking horse,
    tiny manger scene, of course.
A silver star, to top the fun.
    Bring in the gifts and now we're done.

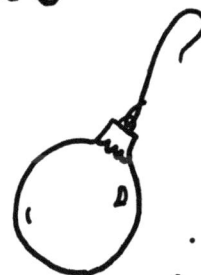

Ten Little Carolers

Ten little carolers standing in a row,   (Hold up ten fingers.)
    Singing in the Christmas snow.

Dressed in snowsuits blue and red,   (Touch your shoulders.)
    A hood or a hat on each little head.   (Touch your head.)

Hear them singing loud and clear,   (Wiggle your fingers.)
    Christmas songs I love to hear.   (Touch your ears.)

Ten little carolers singing   (Hold up ten fingers.)
    in the snow—
    Brrrr, the wind begins to blow.   (Blow on your fingers.)

We'll play and sing where it is warm,   (Wiggle your fingers.)
    Safe away from the winter storm.   (Hide your hands
                                 behind your back.)

Toy Shop Magic

(Clap to the rhythm or do the actions.)

"Tick! Tock! Tick! Tock!
   "Midnight," says the toy shop clock.

**(Clap hands and tip your
head from side to side.)**

Watch the magic fun begin
   with a soldier made of tin.

**(Stand stiff and march
in place.)**

He toots his horn and tips his hat
   and signals to the calico cat.

(Blow your trumpet.)
(Wave your arm.)

Jack-in-the-box pops up to say,
   "Wake up, my friends, it's time to
   play."

**(Bend down and
pop up.)**

He winds the key of the music box.
   The dancing doll begins to talk.

(Wind the key.)
**(Move your hands and
bend from side to side.)**

All the night they laugh and play
   'til light of dawn begins the day.

"Tick! Tock! Tick! Tock! Morning,"
   says the toy shop clock.

**(Clap hands and tip your
head from side to side.)**

No one knows. Only me.
   Tin soldier dropped his horn,
   you see.

(Point to yourself.)
(Pick up horn.)

Ten Seconds to New Year

**(Can you count backwards?
Hold up ten fingers and try.)**

10   happy thoughts
9   friends to remember
8   sunny days, before December
7   good deeds
6   rain showers
5   April Fool's jokes
4   May flowers
3   special smiles
2   dreams come true
1   big wish

HAPPY NEW YEAR TO YOU!

The Valentine

Knock! Knock! On my door.	(Knock one hand on the other.)
Ding! Dong! Goes the bell.	(Push the bell.)
It might be for me.	(Point to yourself.)
You never can tell.	(Shrug your shoulders.)
Peek out window.	(Peek between your hands.)
Nobody's there.	(Shake your head.)
Peek out the door.	(Open the door and look out.)
Brrr, a blast of cold air.	(Hug yourself and shiver.)
Wow! What is this?	(Pick up something.)
I'll give you a clue.	
It's red, pink, and white,	(Make a heart shape
with my name on it, too.	with your hands.)
In the middle it says . . .	
HEY, DUDE!	(Shout.)
YOU'RE THE	
GREATEST!	

The Three Wishes

In Ireland, the old folks say,
You might spy a leprechaun   (Put your hand out
   one lucky day.   over your eyes.)
Red cap,   (Touch your head.)
Green coat,   (Touch your shoulders.)
Breeches of leather—   (Touch your knees.)
He hides in the hills and
   plays in the heather.
Sometimes he rides on a   (Ride your horse.)
   tiny white horse.
He hoards his gold and   (Count on your fingers.)
   counts it, of course.
If you don't let him   (Touch your eyes.)
   out of your sight,
He can't get away,   (Shake your head.)
   try as he might.
He'll give you three wishes.   (Hold up three fingers.)
Beware of his tricks.   (Shake one finger.)
You might find yourself
   in a magical fix.

(What would you wish for?)

April Fool's

This morning when I woke up,   (Stretch and yawn.)

My shoes were tied together.   (Put toes together, jump.)

There was salt in the sugar bowl.   (Pull your face.)

It snowed in sunny weather.   (Flutter your fingers down.)

Brother faked a broken leg.   (Hop on one foot.)

We were late for school.   (Put your hand on your head.)

Teacher wore her pajamas.   (Hold out the sides of your pants.)

It must be April Fool's!   (Hold up your hands in surprise.)

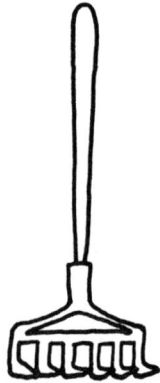

My Little Garden

I rake my little garden,   (Rake with hands together.)
   pull the little weeds,   (Pull the weeds.)
   dig little holes,   (Dig holes.)
   and plant little seeds.   (Drop in seeds, pat ground.)

I sprinkle it with water   (Squirt the hose.)
   from the garden hose.
I wait many days   (Put a hand on your chin.)
   for the little plant rows.

A little brown worm   (Use your finger for the worm.)
   crawls in and out.

And, when the warm sun   (Make arms in a circle.)
   shines,   (Put your knuckles together and
   the plant leaves sprout.   bring fingers up and out.)

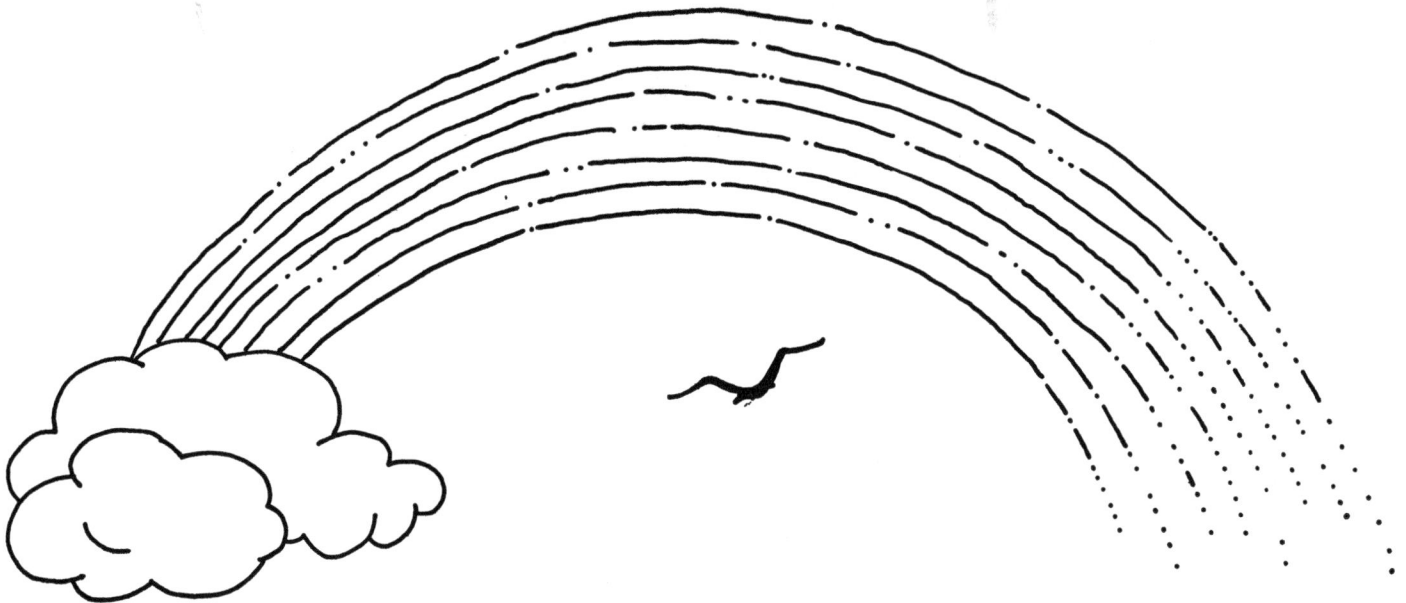

Bright New World

Raindrops falling,   **(Put up your umbrella.)**
Puddles forming,   **(Splash in the puddles.)**
Clouds come sailing,   **(Wave your arms.)**
Sun shines through.   **(Put your wrists on your chin,
spread your fingers, and smile.)**

Rainbows sparkling,   **(Arch your arms in a rainbow.)**
Breezes playing,   **(Blow and push fingers outward
from your lips.)**

Children laughing,
Me and you!   **(Point to each.)**

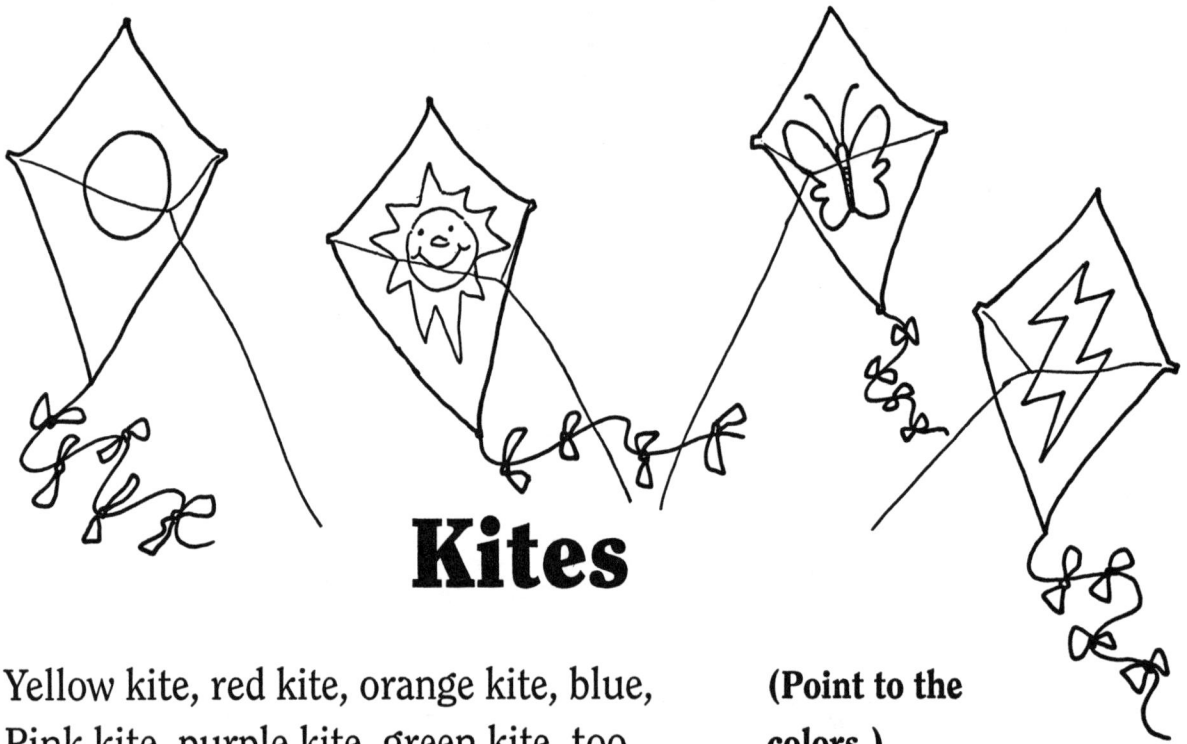

Kites

Yellow kite, red kite, orange kite, blue,   **(Point to the**
Pink kite, purple kite, green kite, too.   **colors.)**

Black kite, white kite, sail away.
A hundred bright kites on this spring day.

"Whoooo," goes the wind.
"Wheeee," go the kites.   **(Blow.)**
Let out string and hang on tight.   **(Wave your arm.)**
Run, run, run, we can almost fly.   **(Fly your kite.)**
Pulled by our kites across the sky.   **(Run in place.)**

Beautiful Butterfly

Beautiful butterfly, fly up the hill.   (Put your thumbs together.)
                                                          (Wave your fingers.)

Will you come close if I stand very still?   (Stand still.)

Beautiful butterfly, rest on my hand.   (Hold out your hand.)

Have you come from a far distant land?   (Hold your hand out over your eyes.)

Beautiful butterfly, I sit by the flowers.   (Sit down.)

I love to watch you flutter by hours.   (Put your thumbs together.)
                                                          (Wave your fingers.)

How I wish I could be a butterfly, too,

beautiful butterfly, flying with you.   (Wave your arms as if you are flying.)

Hop, Funny Bunny

Hop, funny bunny.
Hurry, hop, hop, hop!

(Hold up two fingers for bunny ears.)
(Hop your hand up your arm.)

Stop, funny bunny.
Won't you stop, stop, stop?

(Hold out your hand to stop.)

Stay out of the garden.
Farmer Brown will get you.

(Shake a scolding finger.)

He'll put you in
    a rabbit stew!

(Curve one arm for the cooking pot.)
(Stir the pot with the other hand.)

Nibble, funny bunny.
Nibble! Nibble! Crunch!
    Crunch!

(On one hand touch thumb and
fingers for the mouth. Put two
fingers of the other hand up behind
the mouth, for ears.)

Instead, you can have my
    carrots for lunch!

Hiding Easter Eggs

(Can you help hide the eggs?)

I'll hide the Easter eggs so quietly. Nobody will guess it was me.	**(Point to yourself.)**

The pink one I'll put in the
    window up high.
    Someone will find it, I'm sure,
    by and by.
	(Stretch high.)

The blue one I'll hide on the shelf by a book.	**(Reach half way.)**
Close your eyes tight. Be sure not to look.	**(Close your eyes.)**

The yellow and green ones
    we'll put in the sink.
    A very strange place,
    don't you think?
	**(Bend over and
	 place egg.)**

Under the couch,
    on the seat of the chair.
    Until Grandpa comes in.
    "Oh, no! Don't sit there!"
	(Place egg.)
	
	 (Cover your eyes.)

"SQUISH!"	**(Clap your hands and pull your face.)**

Sleeping Out

We'll roll out our sleeping bags,   (Lie down.)
   and sleep beneath the stars.

We'll take out a telescope   (Look at the stars.)
   to hunt for Mars.

Our chips go "munch," "crunch,"   (Clap your hands.)
   as we eat our fill.

An owl begins to "hoot"   (Hoot.)
   from a far-off hill.

The old hound begins to "howl"   (Howl.)
   and chase a yellow cat.

The cat "meows" and climbs a tree,   (Meow.)
   just like that.

A mosquito says "buzz."   (Buzz.)
   I swat him on my ear.   (Swat.)

Two crickets start to "chirp"   (Chirp.)
   somewhere very near.

We close our eyes to sleep.   (Close your eyes.)
   Our ears hear a bump!   (Clap your hands.)

A strange sort of bump
   that makes our tummies jump!   (Hold your tummy.)

We jump out of our bags.   (Jump up.)
   Run in the front door.   (Run in place.)

Scoot into bed.   (Pull the covers
   We're not scared anymore.   over your head.)

Going Fishing

I'll put a wiggly worm   (Put on a worm.)
   on a shiny hook.   (Pull your face.)
Throw out the line   (Throw out the line.)
   in a splashing brook.

I'll fish   (Sit down and fish.)
   and fish,
   and fish some more.
I almost fall asleep   (Fall asleep.)
   on the mossy shore.

The line gives a jerk!   (Jerk the pole.)
I think I've got a bite!
It must be a whale!   (Reel in the line fast.)
Hang on tight!

I pull in the line.   (Pull it in.)
My fish got away.   (Stomp your foot and frown.)
I'll be back to get him   (Put your pole over your
   another sunny day.   shoulder.)

Let's Go Hiking

(Do you have the wiggles? Let's go for a hike.)

Let's go hiking.	**(Climb in place.)**
We'll climb up a hill.	
Might see a squirrel	**(Hold hand out**
if we sit still.	**over your eyes.)**
Dance with a butterfly.	**(Twirl in a circle.)**
Run from a bee.	**(Run in place.)**
Jump over a stream.	**(Jump.)**
Climb up a tree.	**(Climb in place.)**
Pick some daisies	**(Pick daisies.)**
in a bunch.	
Stretch out to rest.	**(Lie down.)**
Eat our lunch.	**(Eat.)**

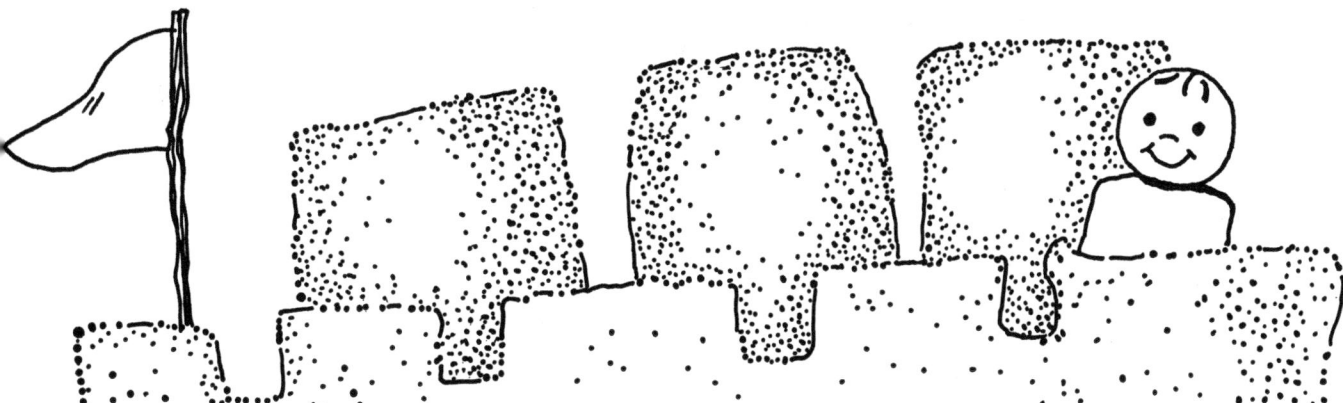

Sand Castles

Let's make a sand castle.   (Shape the castle.)
  You can help me.
We'll fill our bucket,   (Fill the bucket.)
  One, two, three.
Tip it up. Pat it down.   (Tip the bucket upside down.)
  Dig a moat all around.   (Dig a moat in a circle.)
Over the hill comes a   (Ride your fingers down your
  king on his horse.   opposite arm.)
We made this castle for
  him, of course.
Should a giant   (Squash the castle.)
  squash it flat
We'll build another one   (Shape another castle.)
  just like that.
One! Two! Three!   (Clap.)

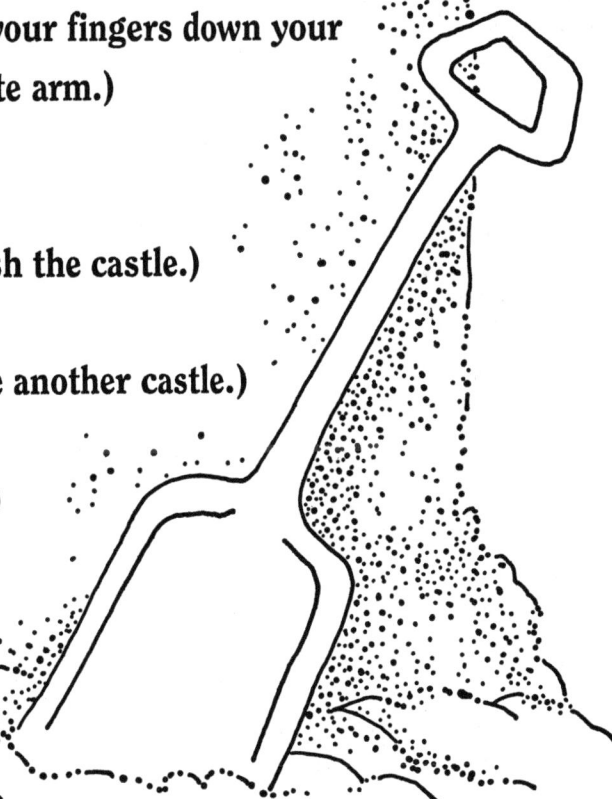

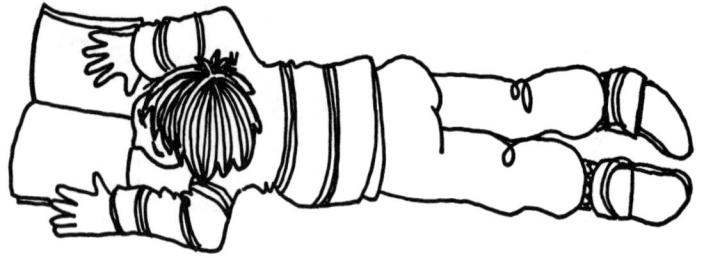

Nothing To Do

Nothing to do this summer day. (Put your chin in your hands.)
Family is busy. (Put one hand out.)
Friends are away. (Put the other hand out.)
I know! I think I'll read a book. (Hold up one finger.)
There's adventure if I look. (Hold your hands like a book.)
I'll ride a spaceship to the moon. (Push your hands up, together.)
Explore the jungle. (Put your hand out
over your eyes.)
    Be home soon.
Try some magic in a hat. (Take off your hat.)
Pull out a mouse. (Pull out a mouse and throw it
to the cat.)
    Fool my cat.
So, if you're bored, nothing to do.
Come on! (Motion with your hand.)
Let's read a book or two. (Hold your hands like a book,
then slap them shut.)

(What kind of books do you like to read?)

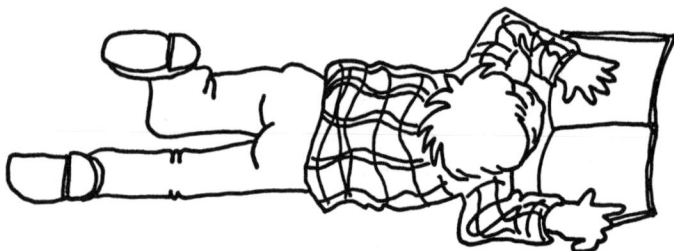

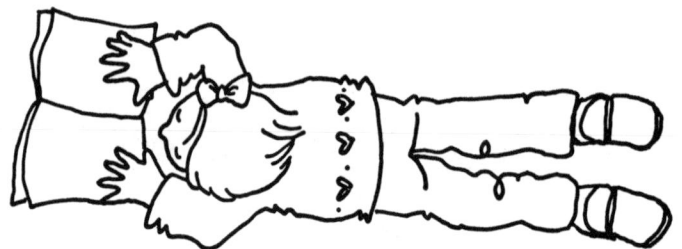

Sparkler Dance

When July Fourth sky is
   black with night,
   sparkler time
   is our delight.   **(Clap your hands.)**
We take a sparkler
   in each hand,
   and dance to the beat   **(Wave your arms and dance.)**
   of a July band.
We bend down low   **(Bend low and jump high.)**
   and jump up high.
We write our names   **(Write your name in the air.)**
   in the midnight sky.
Magic fireworks,
   gold, red, blue,
   my glittering sparklers   **(Open and close your fingers**
   spark like you.   **quickly.)**

Clowns

One, two, three clowns,   (Count on your fingers.)
　　Silly as can be.
I'm a clown too.   (Twirl around and around.)
　　You will see.
Head over heels,   (Roll head over heels.)
　　Upside down,   (Stand on your head.)
I ride my little bicycle
　　All around the town.   (Ride a bike in a circle.)
I can balance a ball
　　On the end of my nose.   (Balance a ball.)
Trip over my shoes.
　　Oops! Down I go!   (Trip and fall down.)

Tightrope Terror

(Practice walking on a straight line.)

The drums roll,	(Play a drum.)
The trumpets blare,	(Play a trumpet.)
As I climb the ladder into the air.	(Climb.)
I take a bow	(Bow.)
While the people clap.	(Clap.)
I'm sure I'd rather take a nap.	(Yawn.)
I spread my arms	(Spread your arms.)
And take a step,	(Take steps.)
Another, another, I'm glad there's a net.	
I do some turns	(Turn.)
As I juggle some balls.	(Juggle.)
I'd rather train lions. At least I'd not fall.	
The buzz of a hornet	(Touch your ear.)
Tickles my ear.	
Far down below, the people cheer.	(Clap.)
It circles my head	(Twirl your finger.)
As I balance my chair.	(Spread your arms.)
Whoa! Don't look down,	
It's a terrible scare.	
Now, I step the long way back.	(Take small steps.)
I swing off the rope	(Swing down.)
And give buzzer a SMACK!	(Clap your hands.)

At the Zoo

(Hold up one finger at a time or do the actions.)

One baby bear cub,
   high in a tree.
Two striped tigers,
   looking at me.
Three grinning gators,
   swimming in a swamp.
Four racing ponies
   snort and stomp.

Five slimy snakes
   give me the creeps.
Six pretty fawns
   prance and leap.
Seven fat penguins
   waddle here and there.
Eight noisy monkeys
   swing everywhere.
Nine peeping chicks,
   with mother hen, too.
Ten turtle doves
   bill and coo.
Can you guess where I am?

(Reach high.)

(Hold your hand out over your eyes.)

(Put palms together. Make them swim.)

(Paw and stomp.)

(Pull a face.)

(Prance and leap.)

(Waddle with hands close to your sides.)
(Swing arms.)

(Make your thumb and fingers peep.)
(Rest the heel of one hand on the other arm.)

(At the zoo!)

I Can

I can! I can—
Make my bed.
Spread out the wrinkles.
Fluff the pillow for my head.

(Make your bed.)

I can! I can—
Sweep with the broom.
Help you! Help you,
Clean the room.

(Sweep.)

I can! I can—
Scrub the sink.
Help you! Help you
Give the plants a drink.

(Scrub.)

(Water the plants.)

I can! I can—
Shine the looking glass.
Help you! Help you
Carry out the trash.

(Shine the mirror.)

(Empty the trash.)

I can! I can—
Clear away the dishes.
Thank you! Thank you!
Dinner was delicious!

(Clear the dishes.)

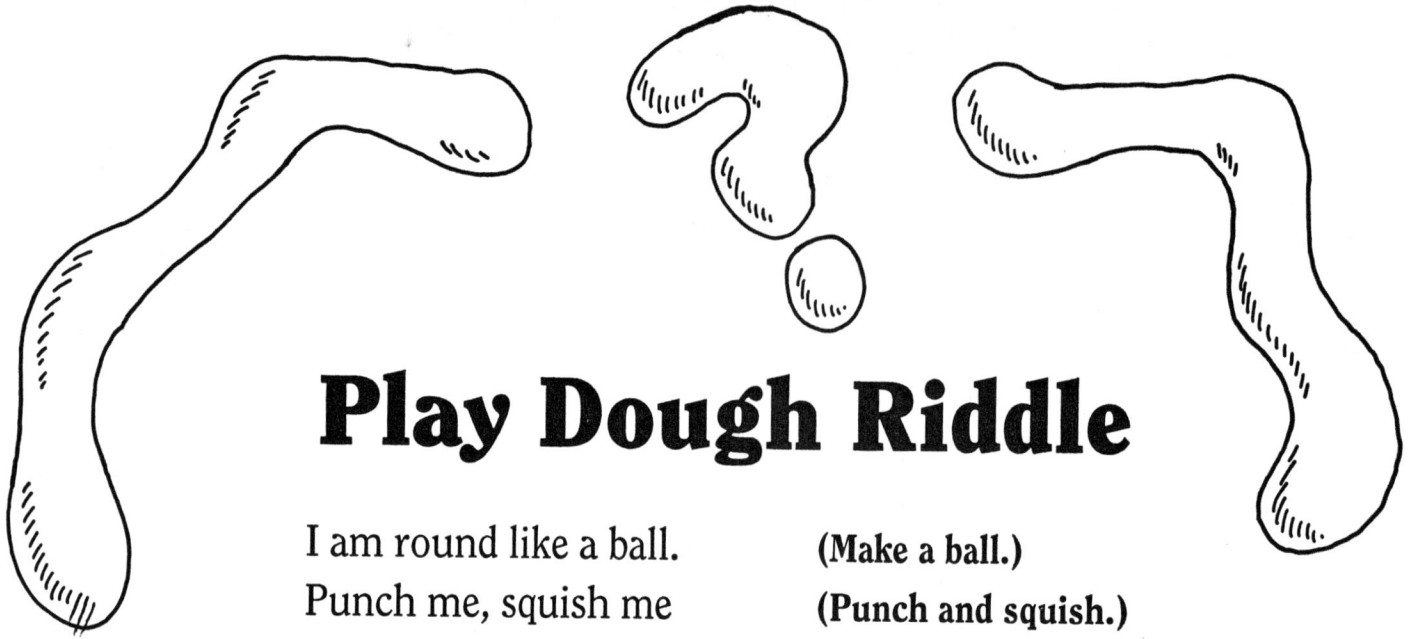

Play Dough Riddle

I am round like a ball.   (Make a ball.)
Punch me, squish me   (Punch and squish.)
   flat and small.

Roll me out long and thin.   (Roll.)
Break me up,   (Break.)
   twist me in.   (Twist.)

I am yellow, pink, or blue;   (Point to colors.)
A snake, a car,   (Wiggle your finger;
   a bowl of stew.   drive a car; eat stew.)

I'm a flower in a vase.   (Hold your wrist and
I'm a bright smile   sniff your fingers.)
   on your face.   (Trace your smile.)

What am I?

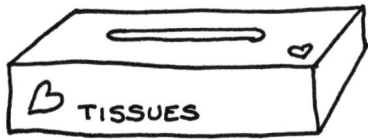

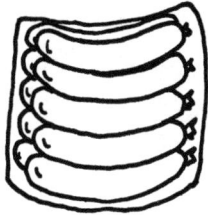

Grocery Shopping

When we go out shopping,
   I love to push the cart.   **(Push the grocery cart.)**
It's fun to choose good things
   at the supermart.   **(Set groceries in the cart.)**

Bananas, apples,
   crackers, meat,
Vegetables are
   good to eat.

But, my favorite place is the
   makery.
It's sometimes called the   **(Rub your tummy.)**
   bakery.
They make goodies very
   yummy!
I wish they'd all fit in my
   tummy!   **(Eat up the goodies.)**

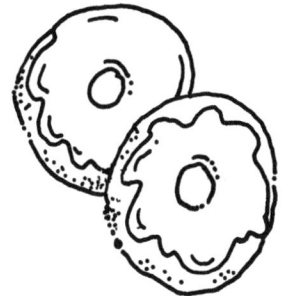

What's your favorite?

Bubble Gum

Bubble gum, bubble gum,
   chew, chew, chew.   **(Fill your cheeks with air and chew.)**
Here's some for me.   **(Share your gum.)**
   Here's some for you.
Let's blow bubbles   **(Make big circles with your arms.)**
   round and pink.
This could be a mess,   **(Pull out a string of gum, chew it back in.)**
   I think.
We'll blow and blow.   **(Blow bubbles.)**
   We'll never stop.
     Big,
     Bigger,
     Bigger, Bigger,
     Bigger, Bigger,
     POP!   **(Clap your hands.)**

Gingerbread Man

"Catch me!   (Run in place.)
Catch me if you can!"
says the little
gingerbread man.

We'll pound the   (Roll and pound the dough.)
dough round and flat.
Shape our cookie,   (Pat your hands together.)
pat, pat, pat.
When he's baked   (Pull the pan from the oven.)
toasty brown,
We'll spread pink   (Spread the frosting.)
frosting all around.
Candy eyes,   (Decorate the cookie.)
raisin nose,
cinnamon buttons   (Dot your chest.)
in a row.
Is it time to laugh   (Shrug your shoulders.)
and play?
No!   (Shake your head.)
We'll gobble him up   (Eat your cookie.)
before he runs away!

Teddy Bear

Two button eyes,   **(Touch your eyes**
  one button nose,   **and nose.)**
  his little red mouth   **(Touch your mouth.)**
  won't open or close.

Two fuzzy ears   **(Touch your ears.)**
  on top of his head,
  he snuggles with me   **(Hug yourself.)**
  when I climb into bed.

He has a small patch and
  a worn spot or two,
  but he comes along   **(Rock the bear.)**
  when I play with you.

When I get into trouble,   **(Shake your finger.)**
  he takes the blame.
  Can you guess who's   **(Put your finger to**
  my buddy?   **your forehead.)**
  Teddy Bear is his name.

Scrub-A-Dub-Dub

(Say the rhyme fast. Clap to the beat or do the actions.)

Scrub-a-dub-dub,
    I'm playing in the tub.   **(Scrub yourself.)**
With shampoo in my hair,   **(Scrub your hair.)**
    I'm a monster. Aren't you scared?   **(Hold up your claws.)**
With shampoo on my chin,   **(Pat your chin.)**
    I am Santa dropping in.
On my tummy, I'm a fish.   **(Pat your tummy.)**
    See me swish, swish, swish.   **(Put your hands out
    and wiggle.)**

I'm a mermaid (merman) in the sea.
    But you can't catch me.   **(Swim.)**
I blow bubbles underwater,   **(Blow bubbles.)**
    Like a slippery brown otter.   **(Wave your hand.)**
I am riding in a boat.   **(Drive your boat.)**
    I can speed and I can float.   **(Make a motor sound.)**
Scrub-a-dub-dub,   **(Scrub yourself.)**
    I love playing in the tub.

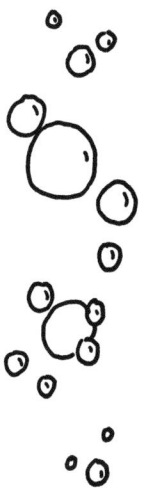

Don't you? What do you pretend?

Secrets

I have a secret.   (Put your hand
I'll whisper in your ear.   to your mouth.)

Do you have a secret?
I'd like to hear.   (Put your hand to your ear.)

There are all kinds of secrets.   (Count on fingers.)
It's fun to try to guess.

Come very close,   (Motion with your finger.)
Mine is the best!   (Whisper, "I Love You!")

Sleepy Time

When the big round moon
  peeks in at night
(Hold your arms in a circle.)

And bright stars twinkle into
  sight,
(Flex your fingers quickly.)

I fluff the pillow for my head,
(Fluff your pillow.)

Snuggle in my soft, warm bed.
(Pull up your covers.)

I think about my playtime fun
  through dreams of sleep,
(Rest your head

'til morning's come.
on your hands.)

INDEX

62